THOUGHT CATALOG BOOKS

All The Reminders You Need To Get You Through Anything In Life

All The Reminders You Need To Get You Through Anything In Life

THOUGHT CATALOG

THOUGHT CATALOG BOOKS

Brooklyn, NY

THOUGHT CATALOG BOOKS

Copyright © 2016 by The Thought & Expression Co.

All rights reserved. Published by Thought Catalog Books, a division of The Thought & Expression Co., Williamsburg, Brooklyn. Founded in 2010, Thought Catalog is a website and imprint dedicated to your ideas and stories. We publish fiction and non-fiction from emerging and established writers across all genres. For general information and submissions: manuscripts@thoughtcatalog.com.

First edition, 2016

ISBN 978-1534898332

10 9 8 7 6 5 4 3 2 1

Cover photography by © elizabeth lies

Contents

1

50 One-Sentence Reminders Every 20-Something Needs To Hear Right Now

Maya Kachroo-Levine

1. You are your own greatest asset, and it's probably time you started giving yourself more credit.

2. If you tell someone you care about them, the worst thing they can say is that they don't feel the same way about you.

3. And hearing "no" is not nearly as scary as you think.

4. Any time you feel like you're making the wrong choice, remember that life is not built exclusively on perfect decisions and that your recoveries are just as important as your mistakes.

5. You don't always have to be right, and people will respect you when you own up to your mistakes.

6. Shitty people will say and do shitty things, and the best thing you can do is ignore it.

7. No one has the right to make you feel guilty about having sex with someone.

8. But you also never need to do anything with your body that you don't feel comfortable doing.

9. When people try to make you feel like less than you are, it's because they're insecure.

10. When your job gets really tough, that's when you will see how much you care about your work, or how much you need to find a different job.

11. It is okay to binge-watch bad TV sometimes, but it's not okay to drown yourself in the Internet and not let yourself see the light of day.

12. You probably shouldn't get a dog if you can't afford one.

13. Instead of spending your entire paycheck on Friday night drinks, consider setting up automatic transfers from your checking account to your savings.

14. Call your parents and don't be too proud to ask them for advice.

15. Sometimes your boss is right and sometimes your boss is just being unnecessarily rude to you, but if you always interact with them in a positive way, it will serve you better in the long run.

16. Stop looking at your phone when you're crossing the

street, having a meaningful conversation with someone, driving, and or standing in front of a great view.

17. Tell the people you love how much you appreciate them more than you think is necessary.

18. Every time you experience rejection, do one thing for yourself that pushes you forward, whether it's applying for one more job or finally asking someone out on a date.

19. The friends who are only around for the good times and can't be found when things get rough won't last.

20. You don't need to prove your beauty to anyone, but there's nothing wrong with taking the time to make yourself feel beautiful.

21. Splurge on good alcohol for your house rather than top-shelf liquor at a bar.

22. February is a leap year, so on Monday, February 29, we got an extra day of 2016 which is an amazing thing. And it will happen every four years!

23. You need to be taking advantage of Trader Joe's more than you currently are.

24. Do not let anyone make you feel like you're unlovable; you may be difficult to love, you may have baggage, but you are not unloveable.

25. There is no specific age at which you need to have a boyfriend, need to have an established career, need to have children, or need to get married.

26. Moving in with your significant other because it's what everyone else is doing is not a good reason to move in with someone.

27. Losing love is better than never having that love at all.

28. High school and college friendships dissolve sometimes, and you don't need to feel guilty about growing apart.

29. Don't be afraid to be "selfish" at work by advocating for yourself and making sure your boss recognizes what a phenomenal job you're doing.

30. You're allowed to have different political views than your parents.

31. If you're displeased with the way you're eating or the fact that you're not exercising because you're always working, devote ten minutes per day to doing something about it.

32. At the age of 23, Oprah was getting fired and Walt Disney was declaring bankruptcy.

33. Ray Romano, Alan Rickman, and Danny Glover did not start acting until their 30s.

34. No one's life is ever as good as it looks on Instagram, so you have no reason to be jealous.

35. It's natural to feel like you have to run away—from people, from feelings, from places, from life—but sometimes you should challenge yourself to stay put.

36. Stop apologizing so much.

37. Being single isn't a curse, it's an opportunity to meet people, not answer to anyone, and not shave your legs.

38. You don't have to make excuses for believing in whatever you believe in; you don't owe people explanations.

39. Generally, if you show someone kindness and generosity (in life, in the workplace, when meeting new friends, and when dating), they will reciprocate it.

40. You cannot be best friends with every single person in your office; in fact, your work life will be better if you're not.

41. Related: finding a coworker to vent to is incredibly helpful (especially if you both share an affinity for half-priced drinks after work), but be careful what you say.

42. You should never let your peers successes make you feel like you're behind.

43. If you learn to make five easy meals at home (that you actually like), you'll save yourself time and money, and you'll eat some really good food.

44. Every once in a while, it might be a good idea to supplement your fifth cup of coffee of the day with a cup of tea.

45. If you have the opportunity to give someone who is kind, funny, well-intentioned but "not your type" a chance, take that chance.

46. There is nothing more crucial in your 20s than having an amazing friend, so don't let something small get in between you and the person who's always there for you.

47. Battling high rent prices, student loan debt, and shitty jobs is terrifying, but you're not the only one going through these challenges, so find someone you can talk openly about these stressors with.

48. Finding purpose in your everyday life is essential, but stressing out about whether every little thing is meaningful isn't.

49. The love of your life isn't necessarily going to knock on your door because they got your mail thanks to a karmic twist of fate—sometimes you have to be proactive.

50. Feeling lost is just a gentle reminder that you are trying to improve yourself every day.

2

20 Uplifting Little Reminders Every 20-Something Needs To Hear Right Now

Keena Alwahaidi

1. Finding someone who will love you won't make you love yourself more. If your source of happiness comes from someone you may lose, you're corrupting the goodness of your mind and soul.

2. There's a difference between being alone and being lonely. Remember that having absolutely no one is not the same as wanting to be by yourself for a change.

3. It's okay if you don't like your friends anymore. Because growing up means growing apart, sometimes.

4. Don't settle when you can't find better. Even if it feels like the easiest and safest option. Because one day you'll find it.

5. Money isn't everything, but it's pretty awesome. Whoever said, "money can't buy happiness" didn't know where to shop.

6. It's okay if you still don't know what you want. Because does anyone really know what they want, ever?

7. Removing negative people from your life will help you get where you want. If someone in your life isn't making it better, then they're probably only making it worse.

8. People will often shine some light into you. Yes, even when you find yourself in the darkest of places. Every so often, people will surprise you.

9. There's nothing a piping cup of tea can't solve. Or anything hot for that matter.

10. Don't keep doing something you hate just because it's easy. If it's not beneficial to the overall outcome of your life goals, then leave it.

11. There are more good people than bad in the world. If you haven't found them yet, you're looking in the wrong places.

12. If someone says they love you, they will love ALL of you. They will love your good parts, and they will also love your insecurities and faults. If they don't, do they really love all of you?

13. Stay away from people who are all talk and no action. You'll sooner than later find out how disappointing individuals like these tend to turn out.

14. Don't forget to lean on your family. And don't forget to lend them a shoulder to cry on, too.

15. Pick up a book every once in a while. You'll be surprised how much better other worlds are compared to the one you've been forced to live in. Escape to a place so far away that it doesn't even feel like you've left—because you haven't.

16. Crying feels good sometimes. Even if it is for days at a time, let it all out.

17. Don't tear yourself apart to keep someone whole. You do you, man.

18. Take advice from others. But don't depend on people too much to the point where you don't know which direction you should be heading. It's comforting at times to be told what to do, but if you get too used to it you'll forget who you were trying to be in the first place

19. Nothing is as good as it looks on social media. Because I mean, whose food is actually that scrumptious in real life?

20. Being selfish doesn't make you a monster. Take time for yourself. You need to focus on you.

3

23 Truthful Relationship Reminders For Anyone Who Wants Lasting Love

Mélanie Berliet

1. Unrealistic expectations don't lead to Happily Ever After. They lead to the Land of Perpetual Disappointment. So enjoy romance all you want, but don't romanticize your relationship.

2. Don't discount the importance of trying at everything—even love. Standing by someone's side no matter what isn't an easy thing to do, but it's incredibly rewarding.

3. Relationships are a lot of hard work, especially as time goes on. But the longer you make it, the more history you have to lean on as a couple. Shared memories are the best cushion you could ask for.

4. No matter how strongly you feel about each other, you can't expect to be fulfilled by your relationship alone. You will both have to work hard on yourselves, too. The more satisfied you are as individuals, the better equipped you'll be to support on another.

5. Don't be afraid to ask for help—not just from each other, but others. Vent to your friends about whatever issues you're facing, confide in a therapist, or read books and blogs detailing other people's experiences. You can't do it alone and the sooner you recognize that, the better the chances you'll make it long-term.

6. Your relationship won't last if you don't water it regularly with love. Please don't wait until you're wandering through the desert hand-in-hand before tipping that watering can.

7. Lasting love is inevitably comprised of countless joyful moments, but also many difficult ones. The beauty of the tough stuff if that you'll grow from it more than you do from anything else.

8. Don't count on love alone to sustain your happiness as a couple. You need more than that—common interests, maybe, shared values, or common goals. Anything that unites you.

9. Some things will always be beyond your control. Illness doesn't ask permission to strike, and you can't predict the future. But you *can* weather anything together if you remain committed to each other above all.

10. It's okay to have bad days as a couple. You won't feel head-over-heels in love every second. Sometimes, you will legitimately hate each other. But you're not any less in love with someone just because you can't stand them for a bit.

11. There will be days you dream of a life with someone else. You will entertain escapist fantasies and maybe even lay out a few precise getaway plans. It's okay. It's just your imagination at play.

12. You will both be haunted by unwelcome thoughts. It's entirely natural to consider possibilities so don't feel as if you're betraying your partner when your mind wanders. There's no such thing as a bad thought—only bad actions, really.

13. Communication is key, but that doesn't mean every single passing thought is worth sharing. Some things are better kept to yourself, especially in the name of protecting the person you love. Total transparency is for windows, not lovers.

14. You will probably have to keep reminding yourselves *why* you chose each other. You will also have to keep choosing each other, again and again and again—not because you've fallen out of love, but because you need to exercise those love muscles if you want your relationship to stay fit.

15. When you find yourself wondering if you could've done better—if there might be someone else out there who could make you happier—try asking the following instead: How can I do *this* better? Your relationship isn't perfect, but that doesn't mean you've settled.

16. When your relationship needs a boost (and it will), don't shy away from getting a little cheesy. Being silly is a great way to reconnect. So stare into your partner's eyes, slow dance in the middle of the living room, or exchange This Is Why I love You lists.

17. Forgiveness is almost always the key to moving forward. Getting there requires stepping outside yourself to see your partner's perspective—a difficult thing to do since each of us lives in the tiny, egocentric universe of our own mind—but it does get easier with practice.

18. In most cases, you'll find that the line between "right" and "wrong" is pretty blurry. And as long as you're still fighting, no one's really winning. As a general rule, the quicker you apologize, the better.

19. Don't underestimate yourself, or your partner. You'd be surprised what you're capable of when you truly love someone, but you have to trust each other. You can only fight doubt with patience, understanding, and compassion.

20. A solid relationship is rooted in equality—a sense of balance between two people's competing wants and needs. As soon as something happens to compromise that harmony, you have to reshape things to reestablish the peace. You have to adapt constantly—as individuals *and* as a couple—to survive.

21. Living with another person can be really challenging, but I promise that you're just as difficult to live with as your significant other is, and that you're both equally to blame for any cohabitation headaches. If you're craving alone time in the home you share, find a way to be alone when someone else is there. Read a book, or lose yourself in your headphones for a while.

22. Check in with each other regularly. Never stop asking your partner how they're doing, or how their day's going. The only thing more important than caring is showing that you care, especially in those tiny everyday ways too many people overlook as time passes.

23. Ultimately, the trick to staying together is wonderfully simple, yet complicated: Never ever leave each other.

4

15 Reminders For Anyone Who Wants To Date A Woman Who Has Been Put Through Hell

Brianna Wiest

1. She's more resilient than you can fathom, which means she won't put up with your bullshit for too long. People who have been through hell know that they are capable of moving on.

2. If she seems like she's over-analyzing what you say, it's because in the past, those offhand comments were warning signs that she brushed off too easily.

3. If it seems like she's overthinking your relationship, it's because in the past, she learned not to always trust what she feels.

4. She doesn't tell you about her past because she's broken or because it still bothers her. She tells you because doing so is a form of intimacy.

5. If you feel the urge to call her "crazy," consider how you would have responded had you been put in the same circumstances that she was. Chances are, she reacted as any human being with the capacity to feel would. If she weren't "crazy," she'd be an emotionless psychopath. She would have been okay with how she was treated.

6. Be glad she wasn't okay with how she was treated.

7. There will be some things that trigger her, or at least remind her of past experiences. Let those be moments in which you reassure her that this is different. If it doesn't bring you closer, it will push you farther apart.

8. Know what you want before you ask her out. Don't win her trust, open her heart and spend time with her only to tell her it's "not the right time." All she will hear is: "You are not the right person."

9. Be consistently straightforward. It's different from being blunt, and it's even more different from being honest once in a while.

10. The fine line between being honest and being hurtful is taking a pause to ask yourself: "Is this something that she needs to know? What benefit is there in telling her this very honest thing?"

11. Don't confuse silence for acceptance. Sometimes battles have to be chosen, that doesn't mean she isn't noticing everything.

12. Don't confuse forgiveness for forgetting. People who have been through a lot do not forget when someone gives them a glimpse at their true character.

13. Remind her that the only way to see whether or not relationship will work is by being it. The quality of love is not the median of all the thoughts you have about it; you can't think your way into partnership. You either do or don't. Actions are everything.

14. You do not need to be the idea of a "perfect partner." You don't have to be perfect at all. What she's looking for is genuine connection, and the kind of person who will protect and nurture that connection when they find it.

15. Understand that she is the person she is because of what she went through. Don't see her as a victim with baggage, see her as a survivor who still—miraculously—has the capacity to love.

5

17 Uplifting Reminders Everyone Going Through A Quarter Life Crisis Needs To Hear Right Now

Kim Quindlen

1. You are not the first to go through this, and you are certainly not the last.

2. The fact that you are even aware of the feelings you are experiencing right now means you are in the mindset of always expecting the best of yourself.

3. The moments in which we do the deepest reflection of ourselves and our lives do not occur when we are happy.

4. Rather, we get to know ourselves the most when we are in the grips of crippling self-doubt, lack of direction, and feelings of listlessness.

5. It is just as helpful to figure out what you *don't* want to do as it is to figure out what you *do* want to do.

6. Going through a quarter-life crisis means that you're growing. It means you are coming with terms to the fact that your whimsical, "fake adult" way of living is over, which, though it's a hard pill to swallow, also means that you are aware that it's time to grow up. Some people never come to that realization.

7. There will probably never be an age in which you feel that you simply have everything together. Almost every person around you, whether they're 21 or 56, is pretty much running on the 'fake it 'til you make it' mantra.

8. Most of your peers are feeling the exact same way you are right now, even (and especially) the ones that seem to have it all together. Behind every person's carefully crafted existence is a whole well of problems, anxieties, doubts, insecurities, and challenges. You are not alone. This is one of your closest connections to those around you.

9. Sometimes the most vulnerable experiences you have and ridiculous decisions you make during this period of your life will be some of your best stories down the line.

10. Often, the impulsive and 'all-in' decisions you make during this time would have never happened had you been feeling safe, accomplished, and totally at ease in your life.

11. Just because someone has it together in one area of their life doesn't mean everything else is perfect. Sometimes the person who is deeply in love is also going through extreme stress in terms of what kind of career they want to have. Sometimes the wunderkind with the insanely successful job is dealing with a serious health problem. Nothing is perfect for anyone, no matter what it may seem like.

12. You never know the type of people you are going to meet while your life is all over the place. Some of them may very well become some of your lifelong friends. Nothing bonds you more than a friendship formed during a challenging time.

13. There's a reason why the most fascinating stories we watch or read or ask about are the ones that involve conflict. Everything (including the person experiencing said conflict) is just a little (or a lot) more interesting that way.

14. Don't underestimate the amount of peace you might receive from meditation, or long talks with friends and family, or an extremely helpful book.

15. It's important to hold yourself to a high standard, but it's also important to take it easy on yourself once in a while. You're not going to move forward any faster if you're just constantly berating yourself.

16. Remember that wine exists. Get on that Tom and Donna train and treat yoself when the days get rough.

17. Don't try to find yourself. It's an impossible feat when you're always changing. Just accept the uncomfortable doubts and embrace the fact that they are part of what's making you who you are.

6

20 Reminders You Need When You Feel Like Giving Up

Rania Naim

1. Always look at how far you've come instead of how far you still need to go. As long as you keep moving you will eventually get to where you want to be.

2. Do not pay too much attention to what people say or think about you. Only trust a few close friends who know you well.

3. Don't compare yourself to others and feel inadequate. Their journey is not the same as yours and their success doesn't mean you're a failure—it means your path is different.

4. Remember that you've gotten through hard times before and it only made you stronger. Every challenge is making you stronger.

5. Crying is not a sign of weakness. Don't confuse your sadness with weakness, crying means you're healing and it means you're getting rid of all the anger inside of you so you can have a clearer and better *vision*.

6. Making mistakes is a part of life and it doesn't mean you're failing—it means you're trying. Mistakes only take you to another direction.

7. You shouldn't measure your self-worth and value based on those who couldn't love you or those who only took your love for granted.

8. Remember that there is always someone who is willing to help you. Friends, family, mentors, life coaches, therapists or even your next door neighbor. Sometimes all you have to do is ask for help and you will be surprised by how many people want to be there for you.

9. Accept that change is the only constant in life and your life will change in so many ways whether you're prepared for it or not. Nothing will ever be safe and predictable in life, you just have to continue building resiliency and keeping the faith.

10. Sometimes not getting what you want is a blessing in disguise and sometimes it's a sign that you need to look for something better.

11. Remember that pain and suffering sometimes bring the best in us; they bring out our talents, our kindness and our compassion. Pain changes people for the better.

12. This feeling is temporary. In time, you will get over it and feel better. You will not be stuck in this rut forever.

13. Remember that you are not alone. There are books, articles, videos and movies about what you're going through. All you have to do is *find* them.

14. Transformation is not smooth. It is often preceded by chaos, misery and self-doubt. Your breakdown will eventually turn into a *breakthrough*.

15. You're going through this because you will inspire someone someday; maybe you will inspire hundreds or thousands of people. You're meant to share your challenges with someone who will need your help and your guidance in the future.

16. Don't chase perfection because of what you see around you. Chase *progress* and what you truly want even if it doesn't make sense to anyone.

17. Take a break and remember all the things in your life that you're grateful for and try to be thankful for as many of them as possible. Sometimes we take important things for granted. Don't let your pain cloud your gratitude.

18. Sometimes giving back when you don't have anything else is the ultimate therapy. Helping others will heal you.

19. Fear might stop you from trying a lot things but you should always try anyway and fear will step back.

20. No matter how hard it gets, giving up on yourself will make it harder, you have to always pick yourself up because you can, because you're capable of overcoming hardships and because this is how you make a *comeback*.

7

23 One-Sentence Reminders You Need To Hear When You're Feeling Completely Lost

Kim Quindlen

1. Every single person around you has felt this way before too.

2. You are not alone in these thoughts, in these fears.

3. On the contrary, these worries are the things that make you the most human—they are your strongest connection to everyone around you, because everyone else has these crippling fears too.

4. Nearly every respectable and admirable figure you can think of (J.K. Rowling, Oprah Winfrey, Steve Jobs, just to name a few) has openly admitted to dealing with these feelings of inadequacy and self doubt before too.

5. Think about all the little insignificant things that affected you so deeply in the past and how they are just distant memories now.

6. Remember that a year from now, the small thing that is causing you so much worry and angst today will barely register as a blip in your thoughts down the line.

7. Feeling lost and listless does not have to mean that you are weak, shameful, or a failure.

8. It is what you do in spite of these uncomfortable feelings that is the true representation of who you are.

9. Everyone has to start somewhere.

10. Just pick a somewhere.

11. You will never please everyone—*never.*

12. Instead, focus on the people and the things in your life that make you feel most like yourself, like your *best* self.

13. Practice the five-minute rule: you can have five minutes to feel angry, or to vent, or to lay all your shit on the table, or to be afraid, or to complain or to whatever....and then you must let it go.

14. By allowing yourself a few human minutes to feel frustrated or afraid, you are connected to everyone else around you.

15. And by forcing yourself to let it all go after a few minutes, you are like all of the successful people who came before you and felt those things and then kept fighting on anyway.

16. Sometimes, the best way to handle being in a funk is to acknowledge that it's happening, refuse to feel bad for yourself, and think of even one—just one—small action that is a slight step forward.

17. You are so much more than the worst mistake you've ever made.

18. This, too, shall always pass.

19. Many people think that in order to combat the feeling of being lost or directionless, you must come up with a detailed plan of exactly what you will do to fix everything—when really all you need to do is just start with what's right in front of you and go from there.

20. Self-doubt and uncertainty will bring you more down to earth and make you more connected with those around you than anything else you could possibly experience.

21. You are just a speck in the universe, and that is freeing, but do not underestimate the difference you can make in another soul's life.

22. Feeling lost can often be your mind's way of refusing to accept a life of mediocrity—and that is a wonderful thing.

23. Some of the best success stories you've ever heard involve initial failure and struggle for a reason: failure and struggle humble you, they help you to understand who you are at your worst, and they connect you with the deepest parts of yourself.

8

50 One-Sentence Reminders Every College Girl Needs To Hear Right Now

Tatiana Pérez

1. Those worries keeping you up at night—the ones where you picture yourself jobless and loveless at 25—they're normal.

2. Talent alone won't pay your bills, bb—working your ass off is a prerequisite for success.

3. Nope, no one will actually give a damn about your GPA after graduation.

4. And no one will care about where you went to school, either (except maybe fellow alumni).

5. Being creatively/emotionally fulfilled is wonderful, but don't neglect the importance of making decent money.

6. You are a stupidly capable human being when you get out of your own way.

7. Your dreams will not come to fruition by witchcraft—you're gonna have to sweat for them after all.

8. Stop chasing what you want to be, and start chasing what you want to do.

9. He—the fuckboy, whoever he is—will soon be a blip in your distant memory.

10. Don't worry about figuring everything out, because no one ever does.

11. You're probably gaining weight from alcohol, babe—not dining hall fro-yo.

12. Just because everyone and their mother is taking Psych 101 doesn't mean you have to.

13. Set a birth control alarm, and take that shit every day, even if you're at lunch with your grandma.

14. If you have no idea what you really want to do, DEFI-NITELY don't blow $200K you don't have on law school.

15. Find your truest look—something is wrong if your wardrobe hasn't changed since senior year of high school.

16. If a guy makes you feel like you constantly need to work for his attention, move on.

17. No one will care who the captain of the football team was after you graduate—no one.

18. 100% of people spend the years from 18 to 24 stressed the fuck out because they don't have a clue how to be an adult—you are not alone.

19. Call your parents more often.

20. And try to better understand their less popular choices—raising you is NOT an easy job.

21. Your major doesn't have to dictate squat about your professional future (yes, babe, you can 100% work on Wall Street with a degree in art history).

22. It is perfectly OK to graduate without ever finding a college boyfriend, or without falling in love—all that will come, trust.

23. Forging strong connections and gaining experience—that's what it's all about, babe.

24. Yes, paying rent is shitty, but it's doable.

25. No, you can't be on your family's phone plan and call yourself an adult.

26. Get a job on campus—it's easy work, and you can always use the money.

27. There is nothing sexier than a woman who don't need no mans.

28. It's great to lean on your friends for guidance, but don't lose sight of the fact that you know yourself better than anybody else.

29. You are always allowed to change your mind.

30. Speaking up for yourself and for what you believe in is rarely easy, but it's always worth it.

31. At least 20% of college women are the victims of sexual assault—educate yourself, and if a guy is ever making you feel uncomfortable, make your exit.

32. Discover and BUILD your brand, boo—it's a lifestyle.

33. Wearing too much makeup makes you look ridiculous, not more mature.

34. …And it's bad for your skin, which will eventually make you look older (in a bad way).

35. It's OK to cut toxic people out of your life (you know who they are).

36. Nobody likes a social climber.

37. Take an art class before you graduate, even if you consider yourself artistically deprived. Flexing your creative muscles is always an enlightening exercise, if you commit to it.

38. No matter how great *he* is, don't let him take you away from your friends—they were here before he came, and they'll be here after he's gone.

39. YOU ARE GORGEOUS AND BRILLIANT — CELEBRATE!

40. Trust your gut—you're way more perceptive than you give yourself credit.

41. Not everything will work out how you want it to, and that's really OK.

42. Don't settle for your second choice just because it seems safer.

43. Soon, your options for sexual partners won't have reputations to precede them, and you'll be winging it in a big way, so go HAM on hookups while it's safe(r).

44. But never, ever yield to pressure from a guy to ditch the condom.

45. Getting fit >>>>>> being skinny.

46. Your window to consume unreasonable amounts of cheap liquor without needing to receive your nutrients through an IV the next day will be alarmingly small.

47. You have as many hours in a day as Beyoncé, Oprah, and Tina Fey.

48. There's no right or wrong way to grow up.

49. Going to college is a privilege many people aren't granted, so count your blessings, and take advantage of every opportunity that comes your way.

50. *This, too, shall pass.*

9

18 Little Reminders For Anyone Who Feels Like They Don't Know What They're Doing With Their Life

Brianna Wiest

1. Nobody knows what they are "doing with their lives." Some people have a better idea of what they're working toward, but ultimately, none of us can accurately anticipate or summarize what our existence is about. Not yet.

2. You decide what your life is defined by. The feeling of being "lost" isn't what happens when you go off-path, it's when you forfeit control. It's what happens when you don't want to accept the course of events that have unfolded. Being found again is a matter of owning what happened to you, and continuing to write the story.

3. J.K. Rowling didn't know she was going to be one of the most famous writers in the world, she was just writing a story for her kids. Steve Jobs didn't know he'd be a pioneer of how humanity interacts with technology, he was just a guy in his garage making a computer. Oprah didn't know she'd become the poster woman for self-improvement and success, she was just trying to do a job. You don't need to know what you're doing to still do something extraordinary.

4. There is no way you will be able to predict or plan what will be happening in 5 years from now.

5. If you can predict and plan for that, dream bigger. Try harder.

6. Planning your life (or having a cohesive idea of "what you're doing") isn't necessarily ambition, it's more just a soothing notion. Focus instead on what you want to do with each and every day of your existence. That's noble. That's worthwhile. That will get you somewhere.

7. You owe nothing to your younger self. You are not responsible for being the person you once thought you'd be.

8. You owe everything to the adult you are today. You owe it to yourself to ask yourself what you like, what you want, what calls you, what you need, and what you deserve.

9. Do you know why you don't have the things you once thought you wanted? Because you don't want them anymore. Not badly enough.

10. It's likely that you're between realizing you don't want what you once did, and giving yourself permission to want what you want now.

11. Give yourself permission to want what you want now.

12. If you want to change your life, stop thinking about how you feel lost and start coming up with actions you can take that move you in a direction—any direction—that's positive. It's a lot harder to think your way into a new way of acting than it is to act your way into a new way of thinking.

13. Nobody's life is as good as it looks online.

14. Nobody cares about your social media presence as much as you do.

15. Social media has uniquely and distinctly made us ever-more concerned with the next big "goal." If you feel like you don't know where your life is going, it's likely because you don't know what you want your next big impressive "goal" to be.

16. You don't need to accomplish anything to be a worthwhile human being. Very few people are actually meant to be extra-ordinary. That does not mean you cannot know contentment, love, joy, and all the real wonders of life.

17. Your life is only ever as good as your perception of it is. Feeling lost or like you "don't know what you're doing" is only solved by learning to think about things differently. That's all.

18. Stop asking: "What am I doing with my life?" and start asking: "What am I doing with today?"

10

50 One-Sentence Reminders For Anyone Who Is Having 'One Of Those Days'

Kendra Syrdal

1. It's just a bad day, not a bad life.

2. Feeling sad or down in the dumps doesn't make you pathetic, it means you're a human.

3. Some great art came because of great sadness.

4. Depression is out of your control, not doing anything BECAUSE of it is well within your control.

5. Somewhere out there, someone is probably smiling because of you.

6. If you have a roof over your head and food in your fridge, you're already doing better than a lot of people.

7. "I just don't feel like it," is a perfectly acceptable reason to pass on something.

8. Being kind to yourself is never, ever selfish.

9. You can get out of bed because if you find it's too much, you can always get back in.

10. There is an expiration date on how long you will feel sad.

11. Tomorrow is another day.

12. Everything is temporary.

13. Finding your own strength is one of the strongest things you can possibly do.

14. Being self-reliant is an amazing feat that you should be proud of.

15. But asking for help is equally as admirable.

16. Sometimes you won't know why you're in a mood, and that's okay.

17. If someone doesn't 'get' bad moods, they're just completely in their own world and you don't need to pay attention to them.

18. There are so many people who deal with depression every day; you are not alone.

19. You don't have to run a marathon, you can just go to the store.

20. It's the little things that count.

21. "You is kind, you is smart, you is important."

22. It takes a certain amount of maturity to be able to say, "I'm in a bad mood but I will keep going anyway."

23. When you feel your pulse beating, it means you've survived everything and you're still here.

24. There is no shame in saying, "I can't do this alone."

25. But there is also no shame in needing to deal with it by yourself if that's what feels right.

26. It is totally okay and valid to be sad for no reason (or for a stupid reason).

27. But admitting this is what takes the power away from the sadness.

28. Being in touch with your emotions means you're self-aware, so congratulations.

29. There is no right way or wrong way to take care of yourself.

30. Sometimes even just drinking water, going outside, or even stretching can make all of the difference.

31. But sometimes it won't—and you aren't a failure if it doesn't.

32. Take care of yourself, others second.

33. It's okay (and even helpful) to laugh at yourself and your moods.

34. Even Obama has bad days.

35. If all you did today was shower, you're still doing better than a lot of people.

36. "If Britney can make it through 2007, you can make it through today."

37. Your pain is an excuse to be in a bad mood, but not an excuse to be cruel.

38. Apologize when you need to not only to other people, but also to yourself.

39. You are not selfish for saying, "I can only take care of me right now."

40. If something is making you feel worse, it's okay to remove it from your life.

41. If Zoloft helps you, that's awesome.

42. But if just going for walk does the trick, that's awesome too.

43. Sometimes just acknowledging what's bringing you down is enough to take the power away from it.

44. You will not be miserable forever.

45. It's okay (actually more than okay, it's empowering) to be able to laugh through your pain.

46. Sleeping it off is just as valid for sadness as it is for hangovers.

47. It's okay to feel like a roller coaster—you're normal.

48. Crying about nothing is still a perfectly acceptable reason to cry.

49. Mental health and self-care are things that you have to work on forever.

50. So take it one day at a time.

11

50 One-Sentence Reminders Everyone In A Relationship Needs To Hear Sometimes

Mélanie Berliet

1. Love is worth celebrating in some small way every single day, even if your celebration is as simple as a shared, knowing smile.

2. It's impressive that you've made it this far, so congratulate each other on staying together once in awhile.

3. It's definitely worth having sex in the middle of the night just because you can sometimes.

4. There's no downside to telling each other exactly why you love each other as often as possible.

5. Never forget why you fell for each other in the first place.

6. Tell each other secrets, but don't expect to know each other completely because the beauty of being human is that no one can ever know you entirely.

7. Realize how fucking lucky you are to have found each other.

8. Create your own world together as a couple.

9. Hold onto your hearts, because it's going to be a wild ride.

10. When things get dark, never stop believing that you can—and *will*—find a way forward as a couple, because believing that's half the battle.

11. Craving a little time apart isn't necessarily cause for distress.

12. You're not a bad partner just because you need some time to yourself.

13. You'll be a better partner, in fact, if you make sure that all your needs are being met.

14. Encourage each other to look out for yourselves—to be selfish so that you're positioned to support each other better.

15. Ridiculous pet names should be embraced.

16. Don't underestimate your capacity for forgiveness.

17. Don't underestimate your capacity to be an asshole, either.

18. There will be times when you will have to own your mistakes and beg for another chance.

19. You will be humbled again and again and again.

20. Invite your partner into your mind as often as you can.

21. You cannot fix a problem without first identifying and addressing exactly what's gone wrong.

22. Recognize the happy times for what they are, and clutch them tightly.

23. Get weird whenever you can.

24. Don't be afraid when the dynamic between you shifts a little because love isn't static and you'll both evolve over time.

25. It's possible to care deeply for other people without betraying your number one.

26. Loving each other is a privilege, not a right.

27. When one of you is having an off day, the other is required to be kind.

28. Speak your authentic truth in every situation, even when your authentic truth differs vastly from your partner's.

29. Every emotion is valid, so don't be afraid to express how you really feel about anything.

30. It's true that some things cannot be unsaid, so you might as well refrain from being nasty to each other mid-fight.

31. The less nasty you get, the less you'll have to apologize.

32. Own your role in every single argument because you're both partly responsible for every single battle.

33. Remember that it takes two willing adults to make things work.

34. Couples that play together stay together.

35. Be your absolute laziest selves without feeling at all guilty on occasion.

36. Eat too much.

37. Leave your phones at home when you go out to dinner sometimes.

38. Tell your significant other exactly why you think they're beautiful, but don't expect to keep your youthful good looks for your entire lives.

39. Challenge each other, but know each other's limits,

40. Cancel your plans with friends once in awhile just to be together.

41. Watch as many movies and read as many books as possible together so you can escape reality holding hands.

42. Make sure you have at least one inside joke at all times.

43. Try to guess what your significant other is thinking because it's fun—whether you're right or wrong.

44. You're going to hate each other sometimes, but hopefully not for too long.

45. It's perfectly normal to lean on friends and family members instead of each other sometimes.

46. Be honest about what you want and need—out of your relationship and life overall—especially as those wants and needs change over time.

47. You might have to pretend to like each other's families more than you actually do sometimes.

48. The only way to know the answer is to ask the question.

49. It's your duty to defend each other's honor.

50. There are a billion ways to say 'I love you,' so say it as often as possible in your own way.

12

50 Little Reminders That Will Get You Through Any Tough Day

Lauren Jarvis-Gibson

1. We've all had them and you are not alone.

2. Tomorrow is a fresh start where today can be washed away.

3. We have all gone through loss, but the best stories are when you grow stronger from that loss.

4. You are still alive and breathing.

5. You're worthy of greatness, even if you don't see it yet.

6. What you are feeling today does not define you.

7. Time truly heals most anything.

8. Count your blessings, not your calories.

9. You are allowed to not be ok.

10. Your anxiety or depression is nothing to be ashamed of.

11. Someone in this world cares deeply about you.

12. Asking for help does not make you weak.

13. Forty years from now, you won't care about eating more than one piece of cake.

14. Comparing yourself to others will do nothing but damage your mind.

15. Everyone is overly conscious of themselves and probably will never notice your blemishes.

16. Don't keep your negative feelings hidden. Talk to someone.

17. Every day is a gift to do something new.

18. Even if today sucked, tomorrow could be the best day of your life.

19. *We think too much and feel too little.* – Charlie Chaplin

20. Smiling can raise your endorphins, so go on and give it a go.

21. So can cuddling.

22. We live in a world where chocolate exists.

23. Today is not forever.

24. Taylor Swift had to get over Joe Jonas, Harry Styles, and Jake Gyllenhaal. If she did it, you can do it too.

25. Being sad for no reason does not mean you're crazy. You're just human.

26. It's not a crime to take a day off from real life and take care of yourself.

27. If you are living, you are still surviving and becoming stronger.

28. *The past can hurt, but the way I see it, you can either run from it or learn from it.* – The Lion King

29. You will love again, I promise.

30. The most beautiful things you can get from life are free.

31. Yes, you can buy cookie dough and not get sick from it.

32. You don't have to be so brave all the time.

33. Your real friends will not think your sadness is a burden. Give them a call.

34. Sometimes all you need is a really good hug.

35. The worst days won't be as memorable as the best days that are yet to come.

36. Being happy all the time, won't give you good experience and won't teach you anything about yourself.

37. *When a flower doesn't bloom, you fix the environment in which it grows, not the flower.* – Alexander Den Heijer

38. If you have a roof over your head, that's already one thing to be grateful about.

39. It's ok to not love yourself 100% right now, but take everyday to let yourself know you're doing your best.

40. If there is a negative person in your life that makes you feel horrible, cut them out of your life and watch it get better.

41. Even Beyoncé has terrible days.

42. Don't let your demons from the past ruin your future.

43. *Only in darkness can you see the stars.* – Martin Luther King Jr.

44. Allowing yourself to cry and to feel is allowing yourself to heal.

45. Taking baby steps is better than not taking any at all.

46. You are more important than you even know.

47. Your life is precious and beautiful. Don't take that for granted.

48. Pain is only a fleeting moment. It's not your whole life.

49. Listen to what your body is telling you and follow it's advice.

50. You are here because you are a miracle. Don't let one day ruin it all for your future self.

13

25 Important Reminders You Need To Hear When Your Heart Is Breaking

Rania Naim

1. Your heart won't stay broken forever. You will meet people who will slowly heal it again—new friends, new lovers or new family members.

2. Don't blame yourself for loving too much or giving too much. It was how you truly felt and it is how you *love*. You shouldn't be ashamed of the way you love.

3. Sometimes we hold on to people who are wrong for us; we may not know it right away but eventually we understand why it was for the better.

4. A broken heart makes you a stronger and a wiser person. Pain changes people.

5. A broken heart teaches you how to be compassionate with others and with yourself.

6. You may not get the closure you wanted, but this is also some kind of closure. We sometimes have to close doors without ever looking back.

7. A broken heart will put up walls for those who might want to break it in the future. Sometimes a broken heart saves you from even more heartbreak.

8. You will always get over the people you thought you wouldn't.

9. Anything that feels forced or harder than it should be or causes you pain and distress is not meant for you. Things that are meant for you have a way of flowing smoothly into your life. The more you fight for something that is not meant for you, the more it will fight you.

10. Every goodbye comes with a better hello; every ending has a better beginning. It's a transitional phase for you as a person to focus on something other than *someone else.* This is when you truly change from within and change your life.

11. It's better to be alone than with someone who doesn't appreciate you or someone who makes you believe that loving you is hard.

12. Just because someone rejected you doesn't mean everyone will. Sometimes good things are taken away from us so we can find better things.

13. If you have good friends, they will get you through the hardest of heartbreaks.

14. Losing someone that meant a lot to you will enlighten you to replace this loss with something more fulfilling and more meaningful.

15. A broken heart inspires you to do things you are passionate about or tap into your creativity. *Sometimes pain transforms us into artists.*

16. A broken heart teaches you to embrace being alone and loneliness teaches you how to survive.

17. Even if you miss them, it doesn't mean they were right for you or you should want them back.

18. Remember why you broke up every time you think about them. It will help you resist the urge to call or text them.

19. If you don't want to stay friends, don't. Real friends don't walk away from each other.

20. You will laugh again and you will love again. Pain is *temporary.*

21. A broken heart is a gift that builds character and helps you reconnect with yourself.

22. A broken heart is a reminder that you fought through some of the worst days in your life and *survived.*

23. There is nothing that time and space won't heal.

24. Every day you will think about them a little less until you no longer think about them.

25. Someone will come into your life and remind you exactly why it wasn't meant to be with the person who broke your heart.

14

33 Important Reminders For All You College Grads As You Embark On This Next Chapter

Ari Eastman

1. You're not the only one who's scared about this. Big change is a lot like reaching the top of a roller coaster. It's exciting and you're full of adrenaline, but it can be downright frightening to not know what's about to happen next.

2. Being nervous about something means you care about it. That's a good thing.

3. Your first job is just that, your first job. It doesn't have to be *cue Hilary Duff* what dreams are made of. Getting a paycheck is exciting. Don't let anyone take that away from you.

4. It's just as brave taking a 9-5 to support yourself financially as it is following your childhood dreams.

5. Things take time. You can't always rush to the next part.

6. Your goals are going to constantly change. Your passions might evolve too. You're not required to love the same thing you loved five years ago, two years ago, or even a month ago. Give yourself permission to try new things.

7. You don't have to work in the field you got your degree in.

8. You're going to lose touch with some of those friends you made the past four years. It sucks, but that's a natural part of life. The good news? The people who are meant to stay in your life will stick around. And those friendships will be so deep and meaningful.

9. Write a heartfelt 'thank you' to any professors or mentors who really shaped you during college.

10. You don't have to travel the world to expand your horizons.

11. But if you're lucky enough to have the opportunity, go explore. Try different foods. Learn a new language. Get to know another culture.

12. Dating never stops being kind of terrifying. But that's okay! We're *all* equally freaked out by it.

13. You don't have to date just because it seems like everyone around you is coupled off. There is an empowering freedom in being single and figuring out who *you* are.

14. But don't push away love. Taking a chance on someone means allowing a level of vulnerability that can be really scary. But scary doesn't mean bad.

15. Your heart is going to break in various ways: from romance gone wrong, from nauseating disappointments, from people you thought you could trust, etc.

16. But each pain is valid. You'll learn something about yourself every time your heart is forced to bounce back.

17. Cut yourself some slack.

18. Remember you're a human being. That means you're going to make mistakes. That doesn't make you a monster. That means you're, well, *human.*

19. You're not in competition with the people on your Facebook timeline.

20. Stop constantly checking up on that one ex through social media. I promise, it will never end with you feeling good about life and yourself. Just block them and move on.

21. Hangovers get increasingly worse as you age. Know your limits. There's nothing wrong with nursing a tonic water from time to time.

22. If you're on a tight budget right now, you can't afford that puppy you keep dreaming about. I'm sorry. Tough love, kid.

23. It's not selfish to root for yourself. It's necessary.

24. Be kind to everyone you meet.

25. Networking doesn't have to feel fake. Don't just approach the people who have something you want, take an active interest in people. In all people.

26. Get that haircut you've always wanted, but weren't sure you could pull off. It'll make you feel like a badass. And if it sucks? It's hair. It'll grow back. It's not like you made a permanent change.

27. Put aside money in your savings account and DO. NOT. TOUCH. IT.

28. Make time for the people who genuinely love and support you. Make sure they know it's reciprocated.

29. Carve out time for yourself. In the real world, everything can feel like it's going by at such turbo speed that we forget to check in with ourselves. Listen to your body. Unplug when you need to.

30. Try to get 20-30 minutes of exercise every single day. This is good advice for everyone, but especially after college. You probably picked up some (not great) habits during all those all-nighters that you need to break while your metabolism is still young.

31. If things feel too hard, ask for help. You're not expected to do life all on your own. That's the purpose of society—we're all in this together.

32. The best years aren't behind you. You just ended one chapter. You have so many more to write.

33. And lastly, don't forget to just *breathe.* You're going to be okay. You've got this.

15

9 Important Things To Remember When Your Life Feels Like A Complete Shitshow

Jacob Geers

1. Everything is temporary.

I know this is so cliche, right? Like, what total bullshit LOL. Because when painful stuff goes down, it doesn't *feel* temporary. It feels like forever. Emotions are often intense, and when you're looking in all directions, but still see them EVERY-WHERE, it's hard to imagine them ever fading. We don't see an ending, but I promise there is one.

There are places in northern Alaska where, during the winter, it can be night for up 67 straight days. But after the longest, darkest, night imaginable, the sun does eventually rise. A new day does come. And it will for you too.

2. Growth happens in pain.

Life isn't a movie as much as it is a painting. We can't think of things sequentially, this-leading-to-that. Rather, we are living all the parts that will ultimately come together to create a beautiful work—even when it isn't clear how they will EVER do so.

3. Failing doesn't make you a failure.

Nothing great has every happened without mistakes. Virtually everything great that has ever happened in the world has been preceded by a mine-field of f*ckups and missteps. If you have recently experienced what seems like a Domino chain of failings, know that that doesn't make you a failure.

It means you are slowly weeding out things that don't work, and won't work for you. You are one step closer to that dream relationship, dream job, dream life. You just have to to summon the courage to keep going.

4. Everyone has bad nights.

We've all been there. Those nights that end with us leaning over a toilet hacking up shots of cranberry vodka and regret. Those lonely nights where we text our ex, have a bad hookup, or do something we wish we could take back. Those nights were we feel anger, sadness, fear, helplessness, despair.

These are human emotions, human moments, human experiences. Why do we want so badly to not be human?

Of course, the answer is obvious—these emotions suck. They

suck big time. But they are apart of us. Shake it off and keep going. Your life is not defined by your worst moment. You are so so much more than that.

5. People who leave you are people you shouldn't miss.

Sam: *Why do I and everyone I love pick people who treat us like we're nothing?*
Charlie: *We accept the love we think we deserve.*

Too often we surround ourselves with people who have conditional relationships with us. We let ourselves get put into boxes and get used by people who don't offer us anything permanent. Who don't offer us anything unconditionally.

And that's not to say that having acquaintances or superficial friendships is a bad thing. Sometimes they're great! But you absolutely must stop blaming yourself for people who walk out of your life. If they leave, they weren't meant to stay, and that's okay.

6. Drama is inevitable, what you do about it isn't.

People are always gonna talk about people. Shit is gonna go down, but it doesn't have to take you down with it.

Sometimes in the messiest, stupidest drama we discover who our true friends are.

7. Money is important, but not the *most* important.

So maybe you're broke, god knows I am. And it's easy to say, *"Oh, money doesn't matter! Oh live your life, money will come!"* but we all know that to one degree or another, we rely on money. But what's important is that you have enough of it it to sustain your needs, not how much you have relative to other people, which tends to be EXACTLY the thing society focuses on.

If you have enough money to pay your rent, fill your stomach, and buy a box of wine, you're doing fine.

8. Everybody is jealous of someone.

Don't beat yourself up for being envious of a classmate or friend. Nobody is immune from a little jealousy now and again. Just don't let envy completely take over your life. Take a step back every now and again and think about the things you do have, rather than the things you haven't.

9. Nobody knows what the f*ck they're doing.

Even the most well put together person is worried about something. Even the one co-worker who has a 401k, nice car, and adorable dog is struggling. We are all in this together. Life isn't easy, but don't spend it being hard on yourself. We all have a limited amount of time, and nobody is getting out of it alive.

16

50 One-Sentence Reminders Every Girl Who's Tired Of Hookup Culture Needs To Hear Right Now

Kendra Syrdal

1. It's okay to care about people; in fact, it's a good thing.

2. You're allowed to want more than just a one night stand.

3. It's completely and totally normal to feel lonely.

4. But speak up if it feels like the loneliness is getting to you and ask for help.

5. As cliché as it is, love comes around when you aren't looking for it.

6. There is no shame in demanding what you deserve.

7. There is no right way or wrong way to love someone.

8. Respect is not something you should ever have to ask for from someone who cares about you.

9. You never have to apologize for wanting to be loved; it's human.

10. Having a broken heart doesn't make you damaged goods or undateable.

11. If Tinder is exhausting and frustrating, just delete it.

12. There is no such thing as "the cool girl", and you can stop pretending to be her.

13. Because you're cool as hell just the way you are.

14. If someone only calls you at 2 AM you don't have to answer the phone.

15. It is perfectly okay to let go of people who do not fit into your life.

16. You don't have to apologize for being "old fashioned" if it's who you are.

17. There's other love out there, other than romantic love, that can make you feel just as full.

18. You should never have to compromise a part of your life to make someone else feel like being a part of it.

19. Sometimes taking a break to find yourself is the healthiest thing you can do.

20. If someone makes you feel shitty about the things that you want in life, the only shitty thing in the equation is them.

21. Wanting to be swept off your feet doesn't make you unrealistic or gross.

22. No matter what anyone says, everyone loves the feeling of getting butterflies and they're lying if they say otherwise.

23. It is okay to want a connection deeper than something formed in 140 characters or less.

24. Love is never something that should leave you feeling empty.

25. And if it does, it's not real love.

26. You are not stupid for believing what someone says even if it turned out to not be true.

27. Looking for the good people is an admirable quality, not one that makes you naïve.

28. If someone feeds you lines to get something from you, that says more about their personality than the fact that you trusted them.

29. Having standards doesn't make you a bitch, it makes you strong.

30. If something feels wrong, it probably is.

31. You don't have to pretend to be a Netflix and Chill girl if that isn't who you are.

32. You do not have to make room in your life for people who do not want to be there unless they get something from you.

33. It's okay to block numbers from your phone if they only bring you pain when they flash across the screen.

34. But you aren't stupid for picking up the phone anyway sometimes (because we all have).

35. You will not die alone.

36. You are not a cliché or dumb for asking the "what are we" question.

37. It's okay to like labels and to find comfort in having them.

38. If someone makes you feel bad for asking for what you want, they are selfish and do not deserve you.

39. It is never weak to love someone.

40. Demanding more for yourself is brave and something that should be admired.

41. There is an ebb and a flow to dating and if you're feeling frustrated or like you're in a bad spot, just remember that it will pass.

42. No one should ever be allowed to shame you for saying, "This isn't who I am."

43. You are allowed to miss people even if they hurt you.

44. Everyone has said they were done with dating at least once in their life—you're not alone and you aren't dramatic.

45. "Being chill" is not synonymous with "lovable".

46. There is something to be said for actually knowing what you want and waiting for it.

47. "Needy", "Clingy", and "Crazy" are excuses that immature people use to make themselves feel better about their own bad behavior, and they do not in any way define you.

48. "No" is a complete sentence.

49. If you aren't having fun with your life, it's okay to change it.

50. You are enough.

Thought Catalog, it's a website.

www.thoughtcatalog.com

Social

facebook.com/thoughtcatalog
twitter.com/thoughtcatalog
tumblr.com/thoughtcatalog
instagram.com/thoughtcatalog

Corporate

www.thought.is

CPSIA information can be obtained
at www.ICGtesting.com
Printed in the USA
BVHW03s2141080318
510118BV00001B/56/P